Simon Jenner

Wrong Evenings

First published in 2011
by Waterloo Press (Hove)
95 Wick Hall
Furze Hill
Hove BN3 1NG

Printed in Palatino 11pt by
One Digital
54 Hollingdean Road
East Sussex BN2 4AA

© Simon Jenner 2011

All rights remain with the author.

Cover image, Martinsyde G100, *History of 22 Squadron R.A.F*
© Simon Jenner (1979)
Cover design © Waterloo Press 2011

Simon Jenner is hereby identified as author of this work in accordance with Section 77 of the Copyright, Designs and Patents Act 1988

This book is sold subject to the condition that it shall not, by way of trade or otherwise, be lent, resold, hired out or otherwise circulated without the author's prior consent in any form of binding or cover other than that in which it is published and without a similar condition including this condition being imposed on the subsequent purchaser.

A CIP record for this book is available
from the British Library

ISBN 978 1 906742 31 7

Acknowledgements

I gratefully acknowledge a Grant from the Royal Literary Fund in 2006, and a Royal Literary Fund Fellowship from 2008-10.

I'm particularly grateful to Pauline Suett-Barbieri, who made numerous suggested amendments to the text; to Naomi Foyle for detailed fine-tunings; and as ever to Club '94's amiable threshing floor. The late Beryl Fenton, Michael Fenton, Leon de Mazio, Robert Whittle, themselves all sadly gathered in; Carole Bremson, Bernadette Cremin, Charles Lind, Alan Morrison, John O'Donoghue, Phil Ruthen, Sonja (Ctvtrecka) Tatum, Cristina Viti, Jan Whiston, Alf Wiltshire. Most of all to David Pollard, badgerer and begeter of this volume.

Some of these poems have appeared in *the Recusant* and *Emergency Verse* (ed. Alan Morrison, Caparison, 2011).

By the same author

From Head to Foot (K-Tek, 1996)
Player Time/Player-Zeit (Zeitriss, 1998)
Waterloo Sampler No 1 (Waterloo Press, 2004)
About Bloody Time (Waterloo Press, 2006)
Pessoa: A Vision (Perdika Press, 2010)

Contents

I

Wrong Evenings	1
No Bees, No Planet	2
Hours on the Beach	3
Morlocks	4
Homeopathic	6
Summer Reading	7
Language Poem	8
Order of Angels	9
24 Hour Dream People	10
Creation Myth	12
Blowing Hot and Cold	13

II

1348, by St George	17
Aftertaste	18
June 24th 1967	20
Sussex Eye	21
I'm Becoming Period	22
Parable	23
He Speaks Home	25
Homage to Adrian Mitchell	26

III

Old Times	29
The Tiers of St Martin's	30
Patrick Garland's *Brief Lives*	31
Decline and Fall	33
J Porlock Scraper	34
For the Autochrome Archives of Albert Kahn, 1908	35
After Bell Scott	36
Richard Euringer (1891-1953)	37
Cavafy's Headstone	38
On the Morning of Milton's Nativity	39

IV

The Distinguished Thing	43
Clowns	44
Descended from a Line of Legs	45
Basking Shark	46
Song of the Cardigan	47
Revolution	48
Allergies	49
Friday March 13th 1970	50
The Suicide's Committal	51
Have an Egg for Beckfast	52
Beerage	53
Saving my Skin	54
The Man Who Mistook his Life for a Hat	56

V

Death of a Socialist	59
Teeger	60
Soixante Huit	61
At the Norfolk	62
Scale and Polish	63
Prometheus Days	64
Buster Gut Keaton	65
The Poet's Visiting Hours	66
D Flat	67
Send	68
And Smell the Coffee	70
'Sdeath	71
The Right Moment	72

VI

ID	75
Venus Flaring	76
O Julia, Assiduae multis odium peperere querelae	78
Love etc	80

VII

Exile Again	83
Satyre VI: Suffer the Street Children	84
Asymmetry	86
Black Sea Letter Book V	88

Notes   92

*To the memories of Beryl Fenton
and Derek Stanford*

Wrong Evenings

I

Wrong Evenings

The fairies of awkwardness
knock in the evening.
It's the bailiffs for the faux pas
as the salmon light gleams
at an angle showing the glass dirty,
streets far below full of mended wrong turnings.

They snap round, start marching up
to your door; the corridor outside
is tarmacked with roadworks
dead ahead, with gas pipes,
their little clocks pressure your time,
sing like steam escaping.

You feel it's your bones boiled for stock,
legs water, this road your hi-jacked exit
from a house of wrong turnings,
where a giant has peered down, and
disdainfully moved on; your little gossamer
cusseds saying: here is a chair, here

are your words back, re-routed;
here's why you wanted to frog-march away
to a smart language that could so
brilliantly erase your broke-veined blushes
the tic so nervously yourself, the light
betrayal of you with you, you bloody stammerer.

No Bees, No Planet

An armada of stamens recedes.
A desert of pollen is a desert,
the cadmium edges dirtier. The week
blanches as it pitches for corn
entrapped in a sterile sickle of silence.

The humbles have voted on pinions,
with their hives emptied, like dust
bowl farmers gone buzzed and juddery
with their spent trucks to the coastline.
Here, take a scoop of hollows, a clinker-built

beached necklace of Marie Celestes; it
hardens off in trifling corners that seeds
states and shires. Plagues of Varroa hover
tight over them. But this jiggle migration of
absence tides them to myth, warping

their fuzz of time, a hum
drawn up behind them as bees pretend to
paradise, bestowing a lost taste
of elsewhere, to let it all follow
in a pelt of dried pollen.

Hours on the Beach

Move to the beach for a true throw of
light you said, in a speaking summer.
The day's scuffed before noon;
azure beaked away in a needy
helter pace of seagulls, busily
ejecting their first year's young
from their cater of a season.
The next sprout menus
from their knocking eggs. Young
are lifelike, but wax awkwardly
to it; an oblique angle to threat.

Sited on pebbles, the sun dials stripes:
three cool notches on its leaden measure.
Municipal shadows cross a gull's,
pretend to their cluttered eternity,
how their slant falls; keeps falling
acute with the sun. Four notches
shifts a pigeon-wing's cobalt grey
to a sea-green Devon slate hued
three hundred miles away. No shadow
in the town falls so clean as here,
a sundial on a fiction of pebbles.

Morlocks

The climate down here's unpitched
by the Eloi cloud cover. We're not them yet,
cattle standing asleep before the pitch
dip below the Central. Nor photophobic
eye-slitting cannibals of ourselves.
Just sliding there on sacrifice-matted wheels.

Like its bass-note through the map
it's scored black and deepest, beyond
any hominid layers. The air's
a pure settle of Victorian fumes. No climate
distresses its diesel current —
coloured oils in a jar abandoned by
industrial fashion. It's when faith was groined
in the expectorant of coal engines.

The pig-iron-bound Northern
sucks me acrid in its mapped flue
magnetic from London Bridge up
the High Barnet branch. But it's paced
funereal in wrought work. Its power
rusts to a driftless chimney, delved
with misanthropes, inveterate
as the tube maps they stub out
through a century of track-grimed fingers.

Down Archway's cast steel spiral
some nugget DNA of hash counters the
spring's aromatic of diesel oil, trains
released from winter with November's
missing, Halloween's oak apples
still juicy in their bags.

A network of stabbed
breath blasts through the echoing
iron frames. The old sulphur,
in its elderly pure pollutant
that never warms us however deep
to the core we travel, from the hot dark
gathering fast above.

Homeopathic

An eyelash in a teacup chills
into a prophesy of leaves
caught in a briar. What tea distils

with its canyons of dregs are faces only
curfewed from talk by the future,
stowed as mascara'd possibilities.

Your lash is homeopathy; an occult rub —
it reads just itself back to you —
DNA's an exclusive club

I'd not scan for portents of the day.
Go look for geyser holidays in spouts
flash-flooding old futures with Earl Grey.

Your lipstick, dissolving, pouts me
the way porcelain warms; breath
heats our underlips' exchange

all subject to its rim world,
the lash a dropped reluctant spell
for off-white sheets where your body's curled.

Summer Reading

The blind's pine boom bangs like a sail's
in August night wind off the sea. Back,
it skews, souses a flue of breeze, flails

the snibbed window with cords, sun-fading
hessian lifted to flack light in. The keypad gleams
gunmetal from some noirish epoch's fling

with grit and ghetto. An oil slick lies drowning out
gull cries. Drizzle falls too easily. You're composed
by a pat late summer you can't do without.

Jackal hours worry small heat away. You inhabit
ever smaller sun squares, blanched book spines,
a finger-tip of unread minutes.

Vertebrae speak abandon, a trivia of tombs;
diffused attention, scuffed jackets' haste
of summer shrinking to a bookmark in a room

where the hybrid of holiday and attention ends
in a moment's fixed smile. You've failed the epic's mortal scope
with a scud away to fast torpors of friends.

Blinds knock the wind's changes with a diurnal knell.
You've become a shrunk register of light planes
a scorch and hopscotch of letters you can't tell.

Pressure's lighter each year. What fades with it
nears the dark of writing, with ink yet more invisible
saying: give up death, there's nothing in it.

Language Poem

Here's a tectonic clash of tongues
collided with invasion, contained,
couldn't ebb back to an oblivious sea
but scraped over Celtic tors,
glaciers of middle English,
drew a hard mineral of words

Order of Angels

Choice clouds no angels. Inimical
to blood or the pressure of frost on glass
they're the compelled animal.
This one won't say, but might pass

to the gaudy of God's will in others;
cites the welter of example: a cry
they enjoyed freewill to find lovers
in Devon is discounted religiously.

A chain of breakdowns led them there, he said:
car, head, to the newscast of predestination,
it's one. You're meant to serve, be led
from causal to this time-frayed illusion.

He'll still not say, but looks arrows of desire
at me, as if I'd know I had no dim choice.
His monk-straight hair persuades me it could catch fire.
Or I could, if I thought he had a voice.

24 Hour Dream People

I'd been set up with a fount of knowing
a girl from 24 Hour Party People
like the tramp in Wilson's film, talking

Scouse Boethius. Her day job rippled
wryly like a backwash on the phone.
As I left, my widowed mother stippled

the showers' mosaics, and suddenly like the zone
Boethius takes Chaucer's Troilus to,
we girdle the Aegean, and I'm shown

just her Cyprus shower, tiled and crafted through
her prickling sweat initiative. She had her scope
vaulted with a little Renaissance flue,

the Romanesque rest stifled with a pokey cope.
Boethius' time. Back, I called your lonely planet,
to console you. I knew not a blank hope

attended on desire, or what began it
ten years back; but comforted with my date.
Then my father smiled backwards alive, to quote it

entire: *Consolations of Philosophy* would rate
higher than the shower I'd taken for my fresh night,
or how my idle call embodied pity, so late

I was late out. But you, dark blonde, your sallow light
body suddened in my arms, slowly kissing
the way I'd dreamed ten years back; how polite

my father's I thought you both long platonic, you're missing—
where's philosophy, your date, your fantasy?
And you don't snub my left hand down your back, blissing

as I gently nub your soft jean-loose buttocks, slowly
dissolve from the sweet, melancholic consummation
to day, blinking the other girl, my father, away.

But not you, your celibate life in motion
who call me brother. We'll meet.
You were here all the time I dreamed; your racked emotion

I spike through your Haçienda street
accent, how even when you're mellowing
to dope, I'd not dare to fondle your defeat

in me, how long this banished calling
ravels us to the slide of dreaming it.
I break open a blank world, start falling.

Creation Myth

Behind closed lids the nebulae spray
slowly, after image of the universe
in a single shutter, its diaphragm a black hole

through which God's speed can no longer pierce
to sight, so fierce the matter is, unstrung in theory,
losing grip of the news flash, as it flies ever away.

Blowing Hot and Cold

March synchronizes flesh. It's
plosive to the labial cut of winds.
Cross-currents make delicate slaughter
of daffodils in the cold snap.

I glow with an impossible yellow warmth,
chapped to pollen-blown combustions.
My grain burns, galvanic in a duvet's
smother and tuck. Evenings coddle

without me today. Eternal as I was
to home fires, I mould round their core of loss
and ash, dried daisy consolations.
I hallucinate indifference, am

sapient for seconds with a cadmium-
veined flare; prick vision with a film of
chlorophyll. Chill stings to blood-meted
heat. I'm buffeted back to slow motion.

The air holds synchronized swimmers,
tapers revived in oxygen.
My skin matches, idiot savant, to whatevers,
the incandescents, those left standing.

II

1348, by St George

Edward conjured me through the
smaller trade routes: Portugal, Capadocia,
to displace the fazed sainted idiocy
of that elder Edward, who'd muted England
to a carapace of white submission.

It was a perfect leapt year. Plenty stalked
those commercial veins: spice, fleas, pearls,
diced wth the sailors. They spliced
the Death of course, tetchy in its
guttural progress. I was Edward's double

purgative. Ever after, English teeth
bared a tighter rictus like a corpse.
Crecy was nothing on Poitiers, Agincourt.
I'd doctored your blood; who survived
the bubo was bellicose.

That's not truth, but metaphor becoming
truth, down to the last yew-drawn
hung obsession, to the last regalia'd
corgi jest: you have the Georgian grin,
the age's shadow of my sword's length
whispering the rust of all saints militant.
You've made your death, you'll have to lie in it.

Aftertaste

It was the liver's bitter tang of defeat
he liked: the pilot's, or his, soused
in a throb of whisky to stretch his own
organ beyond a living red century
to the little black linen flags
snatched inside out over his ancestors.

Flavours: dark sea, cobalt, eggshell, slip
down the Avenger into the sea, like iodine
striations separating on the tongue
the Osaka single malt makes,
subtled from the Scotch original.
He watches what peaty salt should touch
his tongue from the sea.

It never does. The bobbing jade is plucked by a toy
submarine like a game cheat. Behind him, the
Christian boy soldier who befriended the last one
sobs for the son he'll name after him.

But he, who tides living blood
to his lips, never knows after.
Is hanged over
the jaws of defeat after all.

The man who knew the white horse proximity
of his life, how near they froze to his flesh turned
White House marble, halts over war when president,
the sour index of victory winced over
forty years tightening his mouth.

He echoes his name to his son;
who himself inhales
whiskey but none of the bittered wisdom
his father drank in with brine; who stays home
from snatch wars, gives his own liver over to the
black and white recovery of ex-drinkers,
turns president too as if it salted
avenger through his blood,
sucks in his teeth,
leaves holes in the world.

June 24th 1967

Their brandy faces were natural to the village,
long exempt from level toil. They looked to this
voluntary morning shift still gritted with a
geological tilth of their underground.
These potholer kids were what they said
once they'd nightmared themselves
out of earth. But they woke to the safe crust
of their ordinariness, trepid above ground.

Now the fathomers emerged on spent weekends.
Past the pub, their flickering march-past
seamed them into some premature archive; a film
of lanterns and bright questions. They paused to
frame round the stained table, their
own pothole model of pipe-cleaners brindled
in scarlet and white, a negative of cavities,
hunkered down to a touch in a million,
a vein you'd open before it gleamed
a new Mappa Mundi with the lid off.

No-one expected them down too, these skim
jokers who'd never grey their foam of words
and tillage to nicked blood and soil. So come
floods, the desperate tight-roped runner,
we saw them baffling off in a red cheek puff.
It was a comedy darkened when they returned
streaked with hours, days, eyes tenebrous, hooded; silent
at their own part others filled in, to legend.
How some extinguished their day time faces
for those who'd voted so fitly for the dark.

Sussex Eye

The day's lumpy portents shape up, framed by
windows cholera-high, to a sweaty chill.
They're her last. Patients say she moves
among them like a filament heated.

They distend with warmth where she goes,
a last nerved touch before ceramic
contract fingers supplant her.
Her smile thins surgically.

She glances once more on what images
their injury-abraded eyes grate on:
the orange carton, roast chicken meal,
photophobia-blinded pavement below.

For twenty years she was the hammer rep,
last political deviant, craven to nothing
but the violence cramping her dreams so tight
it wasn't patients she dressed but stone.

Gargoyles against dawn sashes, discharge
inmates dumped from another hospital
infused new diseases, one alien
culture too far for alcohol gel.

Slowly cavernous ward ceilings drip in basalt time.
Simple eye cases crease fungoid; a drizzle summer's
mushrooms kicked from lidded overhangs,
spore from vents. Time turns gangrene.

This is a chisel hour: time for inscribing
anger on the corrupted lichen smeared by ministers.
I'll return north as a stonemason, she says.
Incise what lasts on what won't see to lie.

I'm Becoming Period

Somewhere she stopped fashion. By then her parents' mahogany tide
receded past the rosewood Blüthner's blunted piano action
left stripped for the tuner to scintillate in brass pegs
pitched past a family's hearing. She went with
her age's clearer grain.

Walnut now, forever Deco. Inherited
corners cobweb a fine gothic chintz,
kindle red in midwinter dawns only,
striping raven shadows past the lace
barriers of waking.

Bright seventy Junes here, she sees them hatch
at her edges, girdle her shrunk neck on her collar
bones, slouches the last of her midriff pleats.
Now the age of mirror walnut gathers her
in an inlaid rush.

Knots, whorls she never traced on her
young body now eddy, tauten up to a last forehead mole.
'Deco was the first young thing ever: our incising alphabet,.
We swirled hieroglyphics of saffron and ivory. It dried to retro plates
on coffee-table tomes so differently obscene.

'Edwardians leapfrogged us, returned to mode in the seventies.
We thought Woolworth's old hat by design, so perennial in dark varnish.
Still, I'd see in its centenary, not its demise. These mauve collar
workers stretching dole round the corner find hunger marchers
greet them across seven decades of hands.

'I'm nothing but chequered panels. My skin's old laminates
glow in memory. My time's veneer tarnished with rubbing stories.
Just as I become slow killed wood, history speeds up,
polishes its repeats, burnishes my death
to timeliness.'

Parable

'Cough' said the officer, 'your skin
bars you from the tropics, maybe.'
It flared with equatorial lines
puckered me with maturity.

The dark oxygen of looking back
to my boy's military tattoo of a skin,
eczema relieved by columns of sun
evokes my breathless lob and trek

to soft harem flesh in middle age.
What's bygone is a cocksure kill,
occidental answers in comic rage.
Now game-sure tactics spoil what skill

comes minus God, but with diplomacies.
Its ghosts in me itch to take my skin in hand
strip me back to raw service age; its lies
erupt in self hatred's scabs over England.

Now my skin breaks out with new wars
I'm a conscience of cartography.
Had I been sworn in with pips and stars
I'd be scarring from high with atrocity.

So be happy in your skin, I said: don't seethe,
and wrinkle this relief map of territory
crusted so thick I can't breathe
its body armour cased me in to die.

But the dream broke; so did the skin —
a vinyl analogue to play nostalgia on
a barking crust to stamp tattoos in
khaki with a shadow pink in common.

So I left with weals, their crimes untold;
my veteran flesh sheened back with new sun.
But as my generation crabs to the old
stiff with the camouflage of desiccation

I see we peace-bred pick bones of war
because we never doubted in our gut.
So its poison boils out, or spews before
bellicose with mouth open, bowels shut.

We've more eczema, that skin cancer drags,
why trust never broke our step to ask
why it withered us to living body-bags
our leaders prisoners in iron masks.

He Speaks Home

The brittle jest of the bomber, enrolling
porters to seek his mislaid case — 'you'd mistake
it for a bomb' — screens truth with its own deception.

Here's the logic of a local shambles. If I could
finesse you to believe me slowly, without heckle at the end
of such a burrowed corridor, I'd strip the door's

varnishing casuistry, let you into my telling.
Their mustard brew of facts would detonate
on your tongue, but you'd swallow, since I filtered them

so clear, there was nothing at bottom to fathom. Such
bright distilments your throat won't stick at. But you won't.
So I shut the door; let the tropes blow up in your face.

Homage to Adrian Mitchell

Pluck a fresh poppy for a fusilier
where the Draft Dodger's war wages terror on truth.
So chamfer my armour with dead promises,
sell me lies through Afghanistan.

A PM's pride weighs a million pints of blood
the powers stream furtive with opium.
So get me high on hyperbole
chamfer my armour with dead promises,
sell me lies through Afghanistan.

Collateral damage junks junkie and civvy.
A war on drugs traffics Wall Street's sidewalks
fight and splice its residue in one.
So tell Afghan farmers to fatten on wheat
get me high on hyperbole
chamfer my armour with dead promises,
sell me lies through Afghanistan.

We care for the women now their feet tread oil.
We elect them to the nineteenth century
and push our policies through the twentieth.
So recycle my ethics with old Guardians
tell Afghan farmers to fatten on wheat
get me high on hyperbole
chamfer my armour with dead promises,
sell me lies through Afghanistan.

III

Old Times

After Pinter, where we
found ourselves weighing the echoes
of each repeat phrase witted at the bar,
we walked right into the eclipse.
'Lunar lunar lunar' shouted an
eponymous shirt-out gaggle of
tautologies; mooning, we said.

Someone sourced a druidic drum.
Most stared. Where the moon light-shorn
by our earth-rise shadow bodied,
suddenly sphere-dimensioned like
a pearl slow dipped in ink. Ambulant
from comfy Apocalypse it
was we who fully gave it dark.

Walked into the lamps' pollutant
light beat before the girl's wail
faded, shuddering like the sudden stars
blinking at the dim; at the sea rim
steeped up our hill, where a last note
faded us out, the moon's still
gleaming top C.

The Tiers of St Martin's
For Sophia Wellbeloved

I

Blood's heavier in the double basement.
You're tempted to smooth monumental Buddhas.
Its deep addicts you to slow, as blue cheese is a fat opiate
lingering in the stream to make you crave its veins.

And this is shaving rinds; green Cypriot marble,
the slow liquid slap of plaster. Drifty as dyed oil jars,
years, here, we depth-charged our semi-darkness
and watched the violet eruptions while we slept.

II

The seventh floor was all zip; fans
were mobiles impregnated with speed;
conceptual, airy. The first laser imaging,
then chunky PCs, then back to pencil-thin.

You can see why New York rules from its sketchy
high-speed sky-lines. Its avatars, these can-do
juddery avians launched like shuttles,
or Jurassic birds who've come round again.

My blood thinned with them, percolated,
flued through their wafer spans in clear vein traces,
solder wire bright-nerved like a filament
cooling to an eternity of take-off.

Patrick Garland's *Brief Lives*

Brighton's greasepaint soul rolls big
with its sawdust. Its hardened ball
bounces square furlongs of fame

streaked from its jelly. Today's speeds lemming
revivals. Our Mistress Overdone
sends for props from the West End:

like the West Pier, the local farce was caught
burning. The set's antique cubicles of shit and teak
creak each facet of a chair's importuning.

Here, the stand-in star solo stressed
nostalgia. Dotrice glisters flat bangles in the stalls
to blaze a melancholy in Restoration dust

caught moted in arc lamps. Wig, brow, a press
of furrows: as Aubrey, he shambles motley to a truth.
Now he tears a corner of Cheapside, sweet relics

from burnt tombs; bewails the heady cycle
of disinterment, his church bones ditched to the midden.
But there he's miraculous, layers oblivion.

His memoir's bones leap to a scowl; unseam to
where every spent generation sells you death,
insurance securing bleached posterities.

Here, sea-spelt, there's no fathom more than two centuries.
This theatre's brickish cube's an elder. It's Pisces
before tides rise; a town that can't layer itself

beyond living greasepaints on a roll
from gin tears, caught humours, the cackle
of a one man visiting troupe booked at the last trump.

You're our soul, caked dissembler.
The centuries' wrinkles crumble backwards,
leave just a glow of what your skin is saying.

Decline and Fall
for Will Mason

To import the Tuscan light
to the drenched Gibraltar drawing-room
Will bleached the prism of light stone
near to his dismay of magnolia.
Murals keep him, wall him.

Stone's all that's left of the hollowed
British squares; town's ochre heart eaten out by
the termite price. The dust ring expands
but the laid out burbs still commission
him to prepare their ground.

To cross-hatch, tight finish where deep sage
fashion's not shifted its black tectonic
once again. Chiaroscuro fault-lines his portraits
shrouded from its gaze, raw umber
urgent for a walk. These smalls, these people

heart his experiments, back home. Here, ex-pat
patrons direct him to perfectly diffused
Tuscan light effects — more Rembrandt yellow —
through Gib's primaries slanted quick from noon
with no such tart gradations.

It's the same in Saudi, where the oil
dries with his, and, without a glance back
at palaces he's embalmed in Hooker's Green,
princes will depart, he says, for the dust
life of their ancestors.

To be on the drying edge of it, each terracotta-
caught villa crusting receding empires,
each time the town's sump or sap crazes like
his intimate unsold worlds inches wide, is
watching himself dry too, too soon in his own sun.

J. Porlock Scraper

He threatened sense with
his wet origami. It crumbled to a rope
of tattery verb-ends, frail precious papyri
and, from across a damp culture, a wyrd
of word hoards. No devout SAE ladened
his one-way song, addressed to
another feudal editor.

His sweep of us all promised
a heavy trapeze artist who doesn't
care to be bounced back, but
kept forever suspended by a poem's
hairline in a Damocles of undelivered
rejections, blithe of his words, struck
down and crumpled; kernelled by
a fist to the basket.

But I remember his disjunct name,
his emptying gesture, clearer than
most of my acceptances.
Does absence make his heart go?

His singularity's a black hole
on 'no', where he'll not
come down, not let me back
to haunt myself, where he found me,
but in a word maché of his choosing.
He'd find me at home to
his chop-fallen language.

Richard Euringer (1891-1953)

At Café Euringer we're all wrong;
shabby to their rattled porcelain,
their ruined poet, unalterable to the regime.
Still pretty in clay pipes slung near the lamp,
trimmed to Bavaria, his sepia laments turned
starch brown where blood and soil wrought exits
for nature, when blond beasts stalked time for the family.

You bring me here, the Britisher, to corpse them,
to apostrophise Augsburg's tarnished son
with our geeky avatars, irony smoothed in denim fade.
The good Catholic tea-bearer frowns down the cake,
wants no teeth-bared tip, as if the pfennigs would dip
in its acid to sluice them bright with other markings,
heads, plaques, the etched dates of the missing son.

Cavafy's Headstone

I've been sprinkled with death before,
a light covering, a spray of coffee beans
over me, my friends' pre-emptive café talk
to strike my doubts and doubters dumb.

It tasted more of ground obituaries, as
myrrh might in coffee, and it slaked me, as
coffee never does. This anointing was better
than any modern headstone, which lack future

or feature, whose incisions crumble to hunches
more than the sand, or tiny porphyry chisellings.
It's such a grain of talk at such tables speaks me
cleared away, by the white surpliced waiter.

On the Morning of Milton's Nativity

You touched me classically first.
An eye abrasion septic and I was booked
for *Oedipus*, where I winced through fingers
at Fiennes and photophobia, stage directed.
I streamed like the pig's blood ribboning his shirt,
drawing neighbour glances struck for such a blind.

Now onyx-glassed in hospital I'm glad-handed you
in audio, without irony. *Paradise Regained* —
the one without a sightless trope, the light-boned
epic I've not read. Now I encounter it as your
daughters did, amanuenses who filched your books
for dowries crumbling with dank bindings.

My own voice can't darken round text to tauten
its coloratura to your tone, chalk charring. It scours
rammed centuries. I try you through the ear.
Your range arcs its iron attentive line;
a black on black horizon spans all argument
through the throb that's yours breaking in my head.

You damned Cranmer for Byzantine Latin.
But you're a St Sophia gilt -stripped of beliefs
by serial readers. Like Venetians, Turks, they graffiti
footnotes to your certainties. I can't trace myself
to your finger's accusatory. You scroll fire to thrust a
late listener from Edens I can't credit, or create.

IV

The Distinguished Thing

Not dining in for thirty years,
James called round anon to my
great-grandparents, like all London;
grunted vatically that W. W. Jacobs
and some other manged lion were
death and his brother sleep,
who, the one evening he'd not
managed to get away dead on time
returned his call.

Clowns

Men ford winter torchlights across
Bremen's night-gorged river
as if it were an August afternoon.
They're not yet up to their necks
but pagents are par; Röhm's a flamer.

'All their circuses are so Von Grimm.'
Behind him rides November's brew,
little ships slocked by the junketing.
His son asks: 'War?' 'War.'

My grandfather won't raise
a salute save to beer halls.
He bids his ships breed their
littering barges, disgorge his bitter.

British gallons sump blood golden and unspilt.
Back via the Amstel, there's a keg
call, clown friends with somersaulting
dogs, donkeys steepling old Dutch

staircases, broad skylights flashed
with canal-caught sun,
sashes flickering today:
breakfast, mother and bagel
blue eggshell interiors.

Before they leave the dancers thrust
back at their guests their own Golden Ale
bottles, long spent out of Southwark:
late candles lit just for them, not
the tap-dancing magi,
erase all traces of spilt threnody.

Descended from a Line of Legs

Clank; his leg shows its metal
down the pungent antiseptic corridor
whose double once wheeled his flesh one to the fire.

Now he spawns comedy; these are Volvos,
Volkswagens swimming down the aluminium,
garaged by his infant son daily and forgotten.

Veering to some vacant ward, he dismantles
his white consultant self to the buff
paint and straps, to slow scars quickly examined,

stumped behind surgical socks, to a child's Dinky rattle —
of himself years back, embryo memory of his whole.
But it's his son who's almost complete, bar squint eyes,

scar tissue he sees to himself; eyes blind
to their blue-chipped reliquaries he'll now return.
Smiling to anecdote it, he winces rising.

His son will keep missing and forgetting
till he's only metal and memory. The father
would not see him seed in his hangar leg

what burns his son to fly, late, to the same doctored titles,
limping preferments, not the predicted lyric scrapheap.
But the son's legs are blocked out, own no magic cavern

to welcome his own infants. Flesh stops with him
who limps like his father with a pint less excuse
who fires steel and sterile children as a fertile offering.

Basking Shark

Spread-eagled naked face down
in my senescent cupidity —
a starfish on glint-drying sand,

I'd recall my father couldn't try this
after twenty six, hacked amputee,
like a spade boys take to starfish;

and his flesh burnt easier than mine
which browned snugly near his red in Italy.
Yet he steamed livid, and yellow

to nourish holidays with a yes
or nurse his body to a lake's mauve edge
to mirror back a basking shark of surprise,

shocked with a white forked beard.
Such affirmations grew phantom limbs
he blazed whole and sudden from the water.

Prophesy or permission, his limbs turned flame
so I'd have the nerves to summon him home,
sidling past his years, darkened with both our tones.

Song of the Cardigan

My father's skin expresses virid beryl,
lozenges jarring with a repose
of mauve, pregnant with sky

because sky: the Aviatik's camouflage.
I first saw them in his heavy collector's
plates, browsed through back into the flames

of its downing, the mortal singer of aeroplanes
my sad father was, who limned them
and loved these, north west of his time.

With their honeycake rippled by wires,
the honeycombs locked into a riot of *Blaue
Reiter* palettes, this wool flesh avatar puckers. I step

into this Orphic robe not yet for the moth;
holes we dreamt stretched linen receives; bullets
puncture doped viridian. It's his last conjurer's illusion.

I'd outwear it to cover up our deaths;
the end of interlocking weft, the torn curtain,
the invisibility I put on, vanishing into him.

Revolution

Like this. We're like this; she
lolled the word half siren, half prentice
school mam. I was as near Lolita's years

as she was past them. Towering, fifteen
she suddenly stepped out naked
for my education: led out of wrapped

bourgeois to slip into blinding
revolution: the new Beatles —
the shockwhite album of her body

pinked, nippled, nip and tuck of shadow
so sheer up in hieratic kick and nerve.
I was all somersault and skin.

She played it as it laid us, just words,
matting over tight blonde curls. *You're
not ready for love, the new order.*

*But touch me, I'm a warm promise.
They're twin, even you English
for once are a rip-tide of change.*

Swedish, where did she get that? The marijuana
blowing unseen on my father's surgery roof?
The Finnish girls, the German? Alison,

the colonels's freckle-red daughter? Pat's
polo-svelte polemics? All messing in the spare rooms,
a weight of ripeness, volume, parties adding

beards I'd never read the same now; flinching
when they touched, knowing the feel of promise
red, engorging the dawn.

Allergies

Walnuts I can't touch on a sun-dimmed plate
of pewter; milk in a beaten silver pitcher,
fetched on a Deco walnut sideboard,
the one wood my grandfather hadn't planed.
I'm unmade before the self-made:

asthma, eczema, that tart shock of nuts
flamed my throat. Invalid, I'm turned on a lathe
of pity, fashioned as the drip off the block —
my grandfather approved my section of a tap.
Woolgatherer, my Nana abandoned furbelows,

her flapper vision of dress-design from the Valleys —
to Action Men civvies, late sixties C&A mufti.
Flimsies of a child's phase; tanks he reared in pine, turntabled
with ancient oak wheels cored to axles that came off
soon after her suicide, which my mother burnt.

Their craft ran up dangers, spun round me, but benign.
Mother knew only their battery of 'no's'. Not me,
cocooned beneficiary, the still one germane to fire.
I was stertorous, ready, adorned with her sacrifice.
She peeled their offerings from me, slowly, for charity.

Friday, March 13th 1970

Safe, briefly, from the curb and snivel
of school, its centaur masters, all
sage and gropes, I was served

a diligent lunch by a mother with
shutter eyes. Only this morning she
brightened on my button or coltish tie

as we badinaged the slate luck of the day.
Now she dodged my smile
like a boomerang.

The stiff shrub-shaded phone rang her false;
the age-convulsed flex carried death
loud as a toffee wrapper I'd crinkle in my ear.

'Nana died: it was very peaceful.' It wasn't.
For years we unwrapped suicide like a horse
pill we couldn't swallow. I returned hoofed

with a horse-sense absent mourning,
after fantasied rescue from flames failed;
when we kids were barred curtain farewells.

And they knew it. Marked now,
unmolested, I sprang bitter wise, cloven,
ranging for my luck.

The Suicide's Committal

The wind had an ear for the funeral more than we
children deafened by our parents' good intentions
from late March sun rasping rays along brass
and redwood, the lime of acid spring.

We snipped my Airfix from its spruce frame
as full-size our father had from jigs caught in war
footage, where his blueprints stamped flesh metal.
Our love was cradled polystyrene; stencilled,

sanded to a proper sheen of mourning when
eighteen, where being grown was celluloid,
stretching unimaginably in gaslight,
a chiaroscuro of light-thrown directions

in dazzled avenues, like these kit biplanes'
zig-zag war paint. I welcomed my sister
through its wire-wail lintel, inheritance
twinning us to startle my flyer notions.

An Albatross with its diamond matt lozenge
was all I offered as she patterned grief
more minutely, sparing adhesive with a truer eye
for the day's detail. And flew the plastic nest early.

Have an Egg for Beckfast

Voices of my teachers went backwards
to that corridor regression they'd twist you with.
My logic was local, couldn't burrow past
brittle integers of linoleum squares.
The fear-filtered heckle or too-careful jest
brighted on the screen blank face of Mr Jones
before he flashed back pathic to me, grinned at
fixed-smile favourites, thrashed me, played
with them in scout tents where I was the absent butt.

He couldn't core me quite. I read later how he
blooded other arses to a different shambles,
welts inside them. That mild collective malice
of teachers neutered evidence term on term
till Jones was sacked for swearing. Bald, Beck 'Major'
thrilled to gunmetal and muscle. Shrewder in hate,
lust or their twinning, he knew me a sniveller,
didn't haul us to locked-in strokings;
the model of a modern major's sublimation.

He earmarked me, thumb, forefinger;
whispered backwards like a black mass,
a litany of detraction. This wasn't all, but
enough to shut the snail tendrils reaching out
for words like year, *future*. I was their bitter apprentice;
but held a start over their bravado-bristled sideburns,
steeped in aftershave, stunted with closet taunts none after them
bore, like *queer* to their backs. Each crushed me to himself,
index of an oblivious freedom in thick spectacles.

Beerage

Miracles are steeped in innocence or gin.
The florid day presents its rush
invented binary of itself in the glass,
cheeks one veined harmonic up from flushed.

We no longer speak of your cutting down.
Here the roots and family sunken home
thrust us, two of its spread generations,
to sojourn in some forward dream

of flamenco orange, rough lime-wash. It flies
in stripes of shadow. We know your smoked skin
matches my patchy silk and pie-crust eyes.
We steep a Janus of each other, too borough-kin

to tug our circulation to a blood-beat pastoral.
We meet in real ale of three centuries. Ruined families mean
me at eighteen months snatching six sherries,
climbing the wall, singing into the lean

hungry years of our drinking a once bankrupt
family dead. We'll flat-share, freshen habits, a city
where seagulls poise to dive us down —
fraternal skirls to mock our mock pity.

I'd lift you my silver twin from the glass.
A cousin's laughter-distorting mirror flames
where mercury levels flash our pathic kin.
We'll charm and wit poison from each other's names.

Saving my Skin

Diversions are unsung: I've followed them all my life.
Stories, like my songs, should end flowering
where they began. Persiflage breathes a pinkish
grey, too elderly to flirt, more like the rosemary
here dusted in a Dardanelles perspective.
They flare my nostrils with a garden for the dying.
So unlike highlands heather. So unlike these
Turks' single rifles stock-levelled at me and my son.

He's six but they're steady. I've shuffled them
across cigarettes like my ancestral deck of cards.
I play, smoke, once in a blue year.
They took the silver case whole.
It glittered, a flying fish, peach light feathering
their hands, swallowed in dun serge.
They re-aimed at my empire hunter. Time
foams in its glass, breaks bleaching against the
white of my boy's sailor suit, site of future wars.

Too stagey. Their clipped moustaches clued me,
Sequenced to the way arguments here are
circular as my refrains: My trunk in the
voyage over; a hommage to my people's
miraculous scathe — though Bill's dose of
Paschendaele mustard brings me up short here.
Puffing. I packed up my travails, played them
from yellowed copies to ivories with jaundice,
on the ship's upright to the froth of invalid skin.

How could I read it wasn't all music? Some
spy's vanished in the Aegean's cobalt twist.
I'll not convince. A light tenor too drilled
for his grace notes, so enter my first-born.
These shrunk new frontiers are touchy as scorched
noses caught by the advance guard of Med sun.
Ex-empires emerge, blinking states, just in
the swift sunset's cool lavender.

Dusk's three minutes is where no-one
can see your loss of face, or empire.
These fresh moustaches never dipped under
fire; but they burn too. They judge I've seen action:
wrong. My hide's cured with sedentary singing,
witched in marriage and the blister
of inheritance. It's why I say I came.

To execute the will of myself, long safe from war.
So I'd gaze at Mausers all day; their *scena*
of finally. I'd set it or the charade of
secret squirrels to a brassy five/nine, motto'd in
a drum roll for a small child, who pluckily
arches his brows. He's caught it now.
Too much i' the sun.

Too rosy for our own good. Their precision's
mesmerising with no distraction. I can memorize
it all for the Crown, but what I intone to my son
as an earnest of my feathery patrimony:
Time to recite one of your epics, old boy.

The Man who Mistook his Life for a Hat

My grandfather looped the loop
in Cobham's silver-pluming Avro for ten bob.
Above Croydon, spread to gleaming prophesy, he spied
the ruined flash of Southwark Cathedral
point two centuries of the family brewery he'd destroy.
Down, he only said: 'I lost my hat.' And set it in B flat.

My father, true aviator who spindled fuselage
to wind tunnels from blueprints, before being folded
legless to medicine, lost no hat the night
he was crushed to the glider tug by a drunken Ford.
It blew from him years on to Galway, back above
the Irish sea we'd crossed, back to his luck and joy there.

I lost nothing in my open cockpit solos, so careful
of family myths I grasped to my khaki flight suit's flutter
and snap, gingering my loop's ellipse at eight hundred.
No prophesy for the Enoch Soames day at the BL, when I never
noted my wide-awake's spin-off, manoeuvring a centenarian
to where Soames sold his soul for a glimpse of his posterity.

Poete maudit, Soames went hatless with the devil, vanished
to the point of Beerbohm's tale. New-hatched in my
hatlessness I dared no comedic terror to blast my fate across
altitude nipped where granddad banked his malt fires and lost;
where my father floated farewells to life with a Homburg.
My future was naked. June sweat chills my brow.

V

Death of a Socialist

Accents left of my birth ghost in
from my day-scorched twenties. They're
brittle visionary instants:

a halogen world accelerated.
Coffee, slogan red posters tat to gravity,
the way timbre drops with age. Nostalgia's

a sugar-hit, traces nothing
but a wind-broken voice, a scratch
repeating sixties in orange.

It's a copy of an original
that never existed. We effervesce,
Lucozade. Yet our love-twisted white

metal politics, hammered in eighties dark
glints hard through this soft millennium.
So I'd swear a bonfired arcady

flares over a decade's black
chasms of shut factories and mines,
before their levelling. Dreams hold

no plummet, but leap flat along
the printed circuit of the days that won,
a silicon febrile enough to wake in.

Then I stutter it was dreams owned dimension
and a running pace; but eyes open on a plasma screen.
I'll breast stroke treacle till I drown.

Teeger

Your approach attitude. I'd half sense
behind me, the hooded Edwardian
eyelids droop away
the petulant pencil blond moustache
drift, like our glider at eight hundred.

Like his career: still Pilot Officer after six years —
some earth-costed shunt —
fading to pink like his M.G.
He's quainted with a bygone face
shallowed in missing its gene tide
harvested in some marble smiling sacrifice
he missed; some fulcrum empire of himself
won from the petulance of aftermaths;
skid-soft landings, clueless prentice bumps.

There's an air to be staked in dope-taut linen
silvered like this, with no jet-turbling
shrieks in the sky to duck or call
a ceiling to in altimeter-tapped
hundreds, as the decades hovered down
options, the wind-sock drooped to still.

Our faces wind-creased to the sun.
We're set extinctions borne out of
our time, who differently dropped
approaches: spent dynasties met
by the fast-rising bounce of grass.

Soixante Huit

Telegraphic days when television struck
a beam, a signal other to its path
before the digital bundle of comparatives.
The bounce, black time lapse from the moon
still flickered light to a future.

My teens spanned patent oracles
of the west, a rosary of doubts and imports,
sermons gimleting the Berlin Wall
with the false hindsights of precision
and loss, profit margin of dialectic.

Now I'd twiddle breakdowns of DAB, one
system failing after another, a streamed
bewilderment. Five, I held cadmium, a birthday
telegram from my father; later, another from
Oxford full of doubt. Our household hippies

moved on, were moved, bustled smiles
at the next absence-yellowed envelope.
We all ochred that year, hair-yolked. Fahrenheit
451, Agfa-stock films breasting autumnal spring —
revolutions rinsed with nostalgia.

I believed nothing then; kept a touch less
of zero each time. By a hippy age I should
have flooded with jaundice, at their antique
clear way of seeing themselves as all wrong.
Mao dead, I could only whistle, not tuned in

to their certainty of subtractions. Soixante-Huit
Belfast. Now I'd stream it with a second's delay
from analogue; a geometry of everywhere,
denying tacked direction, wonderfu

At The Norfolk

Lulled to aerobic promenades
up to the empty pool's edge
heavy with the slock of chlorine
I'm not ready for my name
ripped from the afternoon's foil,
all surface tension.

She holds it, glistening: 'Your eyes are
Mongols. Are you a Genghis gene?'
Young, a girl lover generally,
she laughs at my hunkered-up stare.
But she's not put her face to bed for days,
ornate to its shave and kohl wounds
scrubbed with her day, minding this bleached hollow.

'No-one will come. I'll shut. Swim naked
if you like. Go on.' Pisces, she solemnizes
words with a touch, to heal my year-peeled skin,
cauterize the old caked version.
She's seen me hump and plunge for months.

Now she's more rapid than a blink.
It unsheathes my eyes for her:
Mongol, Downs she once thought.
She'll see how far my skin comes
locked into her panopticon life
all this time unknowing, now swimming
stripped for her decision.

Scale and Polish

Hedgehogs… wee spikes. She squirmed
it up at me on the needle tip, flushed
it down the sink's scooped melon.

Bath eyes spiked out of kohl, stared almost
sex behind the orthodontist's mask.
I should've chosen crazy paving.

She did remember who her words once were,
school kids she'd not have fleered
with the hack and land scrape of her trade.

For me with good teeth there's still bone
recession, relics loosening, warnings in porcelain;
stones of Venice in peril.

Prometheus Days

The avenues of pain dart
generously, fan to so many
founts of unlearning.

Like an earwig to listening
what flickers in my lower gut, thins
me to a transparency, is just a

glistening tapeworm of pain,
wriggled on a petri dish.
It sharpens to a bamboo.

Stabs pester, pacify with a font
of drugs, accelerators of all
following selves to eighty.

I make them criminal faces,
morose inheritor, squalor
smiling on a monument.

But here I lie clean, no sweat
for not taking thought
for a clear day.

Buster Gut Keaton

There's me, there's the pain directing me
on hiss-flick celluloid. Unguents steal
across in colour from another century.
There's a Siamese half-separation
you hope succeeds, leaving the pained twin,
lightning rod of all shock treatment I'll ever earth.

Fennel, ginger, dill peel from their husks
of words to purge me in their originals,
a fire-veined idiom, slivered ivory
through the dawn, inflamed flush of my gut
to bring back night. It's what I imagine silence is

without the comic rushes pain flits
across in its black and white stark and stab
where I can watch myself gyrating
tufted; mad egg-white eyes
ruffle spasm,. It laps high-rises on and on
over relief's dissolving scaffolding.

No subtitles break the perfect mime.
Just language pared to the bitter herb is any use
its litanies full of emetic laughter.
My howl's noiseless as a clown's
who blanks his kohl vision of The End as sleep:
a black card, perilously held in place.

The Poet's Visiting Hours

Knowing how
phonemes crash

on the beach rim
flashes of my retina,

he speaks
in slow couplets

to stop shadows
lengthening over my eyes

D Flat

Unlicensed, I parked my mother's white Beetle
next the acrid atelier, asked room prices,
returned to it vanished. Such treacle
I swam through: glottal French faces

mewed to admonish accent. A film crew
had borrowed it for their set. Back in two hours.
I'd no passport, possessions *passim*, drew
keener corrections, the accent I was taken for

as I blurted my stripped identity
jangled bad consonants on piano wire.
Somewhere, all French pianists played in bright D.
I'm always D flat, Fauré-ruminant, just aspire

to my home keys. Regards, to the barman. Again, I drew
my one rucksacked possession, my moleskine.
Then he spoke transatlantic, blew
a kiss, promised to make me grin

French, till the Beetle was ranched.
But it was asparagus cream
in the sixties: my subconscious blanched
me in a panic scald of steam.

Think you're dreaming? Phone your mother.
Nonchalant, she counselled trust and drink.
Dreams set up with each other.
You're absinthe and white pages, so think:

you boil in your own ditched water
under an obsidian lid; drink
where D is day, impossible D sharp hereafter.
Write flat, halting: when we've done with you, you blink.

Send

The mask salutes its flesh.
My clothes subject me to used slump
questions in a hasty corner.
Daylight's seamed over with jeans'

universal panacea. Eased off,
I've only the sump of naked.
Odd socks breed in slumber
regions of this recession.

Stasis is the singleton's disease.
No other's dust settles or irritates in
the dorm hallucinated one-beds
over this hanging participle of Brighton.

Commuting, I tag in line for my
tracers, lacking common sense —
that encryption at three to plastic
instincts I'm too late too know

I've missed, cloistered in
a priest hole with broadband.
It aligns us to London, the world's
humming necropoli, each sunk

in silicon, home working or tubing
High Barnet, frontal lobe singing.
We tune in, over the dirty forks
we failed to impress with.

Who'd know when so many stopped
transmitting cell lives, suddenly,
as when a cable severs screens
to silence, and bird song bounces

its bundle of call signals to fear-
metalled ears, who know a dawn
chorus only when broadcast
on dead stations' frequencies.

And Smell the Coffee

Ritual grooves addiction. It's a corner
to unchaos you to a platonic trace
before its fix knurls you ever tighter.
You machine yourself to a shining face:

the chromed coffee pot we once drew from —
kids' noses stretch pocked in its pitted gleam.
We've lost its alluvial grouts and fathom
to a fingernail slashing the taut foil drum

of trapped Columbian, punching aroma
through decades of your nostrils' flare for bitter.
I rush in to repeat our self-parody, sure
you'll laugh we're in our senses' skewer.

If this slow lineage of repeats could post
around the roomy might-haves of the brain
we'd not snare the neural maps that host
the words for again, again, again.

'Sdeath

February and suicide shrivel in the gutter.
Its grisaille light backs lemon sun
usurped in a march of magenta stripes.
Slowly the weather frisks, playful as cubs with teeth.

So days can nip, make you smart, let old blood flow or
beckon to new wounds scored as joys. Self-harm month.
However hours tiger themselves down June avenues,
deviant, illusory, they start you running.

But when I'd look back at winter's grainy days
where I dazzled blind in my abraded eyes,
smarting photophobia, zig-zag shutting my lids,
I wasn't staring from my warranted hospital bed

at two drowning in December's grey emulsion
who in my zebra blind life I never called to.
In St Lucy's midnight clear, numbed in steady sight,
they froze this eyeless shadow play at once and ever.

The Right Moment

Outside, I could see Death was hurt
or disappointed. *I waited for you years
to take joy in this wild party, but
you've held back till it's end-nigh over.*

He waived my abashment with a blue-white palm,
translucent, saintly in moonlight.
*It'll be eons till those little vectors come again
somewhere to complete you. We'll have to wait.*

VI

ID

You said: the clitoris is the best argument
for intelligent design, but the devout
won't swallow it or woman's gift over nature
with no closed season on self-pleasurers.

For the post modern there's a shiver too —
bodies aren't ironic, however you
pierce them with scorn for the voyeur,
lust says back to the sweet skin sinner.

It's between me and your allure;
relax to it, only lust answers.
Your voice sashays between the camp
of licence and Leviticus and red lamps.

A burst fig for words that abuse the tongue
formed for other silent missions.

Venus Flaring

On the cusp of woodsmoke's equinox,
grey blue Michaelmas, I read out by lot his
Mandelstam translation. Then he called till
1am those who relayed this to me, haggard of sleep.

Then bolted to wander Vauxhall from a flare
of followers, tracked through a star-keyed rosary
of mobile numbers to a hospital, blank-faced
at this balance of light and dark.

Next day, today, his voice bass-commands
the radio, the punting Oxford Adonis
another recalls, now almost posthumous,
the body-salt of prior recording.

The strange today of the trembling scales
we've entered, sending them flying. His refining
mind's AWOL is the fifth flung this month at me,
I say to my conscience, Cristina,

angel tag pursuer, log chaser of these, the night-
streamed and their calls. Born a trine away, she says —
can tune in without burning more than obliquely.
When coincidences cease, worry; she says.

Solstice marks your birthday soon,
wry traveller of dark to the light countries
Cristina reverses to London. You heard me
open these moth blind proceedings

in flare-leafed Hove. You saw the orange
eighties empty chair, where the other frantic's
distress bared itself to me, then your parents,
at 1am. Hove, London. I'm enchased

with their light, a tarnished silver
heirloom I never owned to. No full moon
spans these wafer-looking lunacies,
wild translators of themselves.

Their honeycombed voices multiply,
the myriad dry eyes of bees; resolve,
in this Russianist's radio words, a lustrous
boom more lucid than recurrence,

a chance lyric snatch at sticky threads,
wicks smeared at Harvest, half and half
decommissioned, waiting for tinder
fingers to feed them blackening

to swart question marks, a filament
of smoke, speech cartooned; dreams
caged too slowly. Their charcoal and chalk
seasons on the mirror edge of this

steel blue festival have stripped
the stickiness of metaphor. You alone
smile me back to buzz and touch.
They're looking up.

Some of their number know me too tightly,
and I can't burn away their bone
bleached clarity. They swarm, find
me a drained comb, fill my hollow words.

O Julia, Assiduae multis odium peperere querelae
Propertius 2:18a

The Romano-British poet phones me
with curses she's folded in pewter
for Sulis Minerva, thrown into the fifty mineral
hot springs. Can't I divine them? Can't I
guess the works of her nonagenarian spouse
were stolen; like his tricky cataracts
removed today. So he's no longer Sulis's
blank-eyed prophet whose pallor
scathes limestone-infused calico?

How, I ask? With the razored strigil
your skin's scraped with by slaves.
They'd flay you open quicker than
any flint knap unpelts a deer.

I'd unravel her curses, see if my name's
incised by her scriptus, counter with
two notched silver coins of the late third century.
Decades back, I'd have died her favour
to enjoy. Now she's ancient history —
but which? Not Wife of Bath
with a face of rose veal.
Nor walking today's levels. She sinks a ghostly
three metres down, is dosed from her
lateral mind, unmeridianed.

It's blowing north-east. She might
find me with her split versions in the cellarage.
She could be translated there, I fool
myself. Whole, writing in elegiacs,
Catullus a neighbour memory, Propertius
to pester her. But even they're two scratched
centuries back, from her coin's date,
rolled into clean corrupted
copies of themselves.

Her skin's suffering now, writhing
on a sacrificial plinth, the viscera
burnt millennia back then. She can't be brought
out of time, or thrust back in: her pewter roll
justles an ivory clasp knife. Pointedly she greets
my birthday as a curse; wills its
eternal silted recurrences without me.

Love etc

There's no Welsh for orgasm — that conjugate
language that's my mother's tongue

she told me. That the Dublin nurse quizzed her fill
in a home visit whisper: *did ya feel a t'rill?*

probing the throaty colloquial through the gap
in her teeth where the Gaelic whistled a gulp

empty. It's the space between *Eros*,
Agape. For the Anglo-Saxons, *love*, the caress

for what you possess, *lust*, desire
for what's not yours, the taking words men wore,

like mucus opals, hardening to horses.
Love, fragile *amore* sucks or shivers

through the teeth. Women with a breath
inspire children they can't own from death

but blow through with warm earth —
had to insinuate through their teeth

introduce their tongue to common men
and hope love's palate might harden.

VII

Exile Again

What — with my face greenish, red tongue
popping like an olive's stuffed pepper —
did I earn this rustic setting for this time?

Was it your skin white as goat's milk,
sucking the Pan out of me
as if I was a bestial-pointed swain

your kin had whooped on
caught dying inside you on
some fashion-deserted beach,

more sand than sense running to barbaric
mountains? Now I'll pay, in spasms
throwing good deaths after bad.

Satyre VI: Suffer the Street Children

They had to go. Those swart burghers said
they traced the plague to its black head
in Blackfriars jails. Its miasma stirred
round St Paul's; urchins, tenantless blackbirds,
each small shrunk head a roving pimple, darkened,
fastens on you, a fly blown on whiskery mutton.

Was this truth fetched from Bridewell's fester pit
where a child's the limbeck to distil it
more virulent in decay than a brawn man?
It sweeps fifty in a hot day. Their pale bodies can
putrefy, vanish to a brittle of bone dust
as if they'd been a wretched dream of lust
Southwark-begotten and dropped by the river
forgotten in dawn by their chill whore dreamer.

Have I been cozened at last by peers? These Duty Boys
in hundreds deported to breathe a new ahoy,
a new world where cried streets were forests
with stripe dazzle, birds' clean calling breasts.
So few, I heard, have blazed that far. I've gauged
nearly all are dead; some plagued, some lashes plagued.
My complicity feeds their putrefaction,
new fashions in death; pig-stuck native actions,
but more, their masters. Sad charted discoverers,
they're more skeletal-eloquent by far
than we, to breathe through wordy palimpsests
to ink new coasts. They mapped us articulate
in broken lines of ivory; shrieked silence
from sapphire birds; their souls spent in black pence.

We whistle through the bones of others.
I've cried up a new America in theirs
cuttled with a reef of them built of a found land
we tie fat barques to, and sea-booted stand.
I'll chart this calcined promontory; this gift
new scratched, new scratched again, to stuff each rift
of paper, fed with printer's ink
down all our vellum-lying maws till we sink
vomiting, die black of the brass hope
their proof was; bright children blackened on the rope.

Asymmetry

We live in a symmetry of attrition.
There's no language for it, or for the
answering patterns outside Khayam's.

Who'd believe he could turn algebra
to solid geometry, solve cubic equations
with Al-Haytham's conic sections

of mirrors? Only such a brilliant squint
could bend the light on such a scimitar of now.
They just flashed into his quatrains.

Here, Christian sides with Damascene
against the rhythm of their common foe, north:
the Seljuks who first unbalanced it all,

and their Outremer copper mirror:
over-mailed crusaders, linked to them
in a barter of steel thread treaties.

Their women banter openly in the street,
are rumoured archers, yet own no door
opposite. Can raise voices, but whose

husband priests were forced to sell them
to their pope, do homage to his flesh-
exclusive brothels. Desire's a furtive zero

their scholars shun, yet begets their
shuddering number. Mirrors snuff us
so exactly with our shadow self;

we can't touch it till we rust their surface
with our fingers, till their silver
crusts our answering face with plague.

Their polished light dazzles,
darkens me back
to the blind algebra of my dreams.

What tight music of reason can I open
to equate it, when kettledrums drown the silent-
seasoned oud? There's a geometry of zero

of minus in the stars beyond my tarnished
astrolabe, with its verdegris constellations
to plot this Christian-cancelling vacuum.

Perhaps I could, through the shaft of Sagittarius'
future-pointing arrow. Or polish a hard-wearing
jet mosaic — night's floor — to plot

the x of each star's picked-out wave, and brave the tide
of its calculus. I'd save libraries from such a
hell-fire-storm — as last century in Baghdad —

breaking over them in liquid fire: Seljuks,
those Shia-expelling Sunnis. Such asymmetry
will invite the Christians next century.

Already they think stone cones aspire to God.
They'll steal our glint prisms, twist them
to trajectories of steel and lies.

Before then, we must beard the
equation; get up all thought
in a caravanserai

so we can port it fold on fold
so the stars can read it back to us
and wait, patient, as we stumble on.

Black Sea Letter Book V

My bronzed exilic face turns
to a fat monument, scoured by spindrift.
I'm weathering worse than Augustus;
his clement features stamp so many
respected chances to endure: a porous nose
in the Namibian desert, to a Gaulish toe in granite.
In Tomis it'd blacken, with what hatred salt
eats into stone.

More blue moons here than usual.
This sea must run off the edge of the world
on the far side; the river's freshwater
freezes into the bay. It's the Styx's
local tributary, where oblivion meanders
down to kill shellfish.

Imagine me altered; my voice, once honeyed
to shiver others to a cry, rasps to
barbaric glottals by spume's eternal vinegar.
I'm morphing to a saline sarcophagus,
a mythic shift I never mapped to cast
myself in. Bronze where it whips, a north
wind gleam, green where sickness festers, a sour
ablation caked in furrows and channels of decay.
In sun it alternates in chestnut and turquoise
sky. Talk threads to confidences; wine-stained
marble sprawls away. Nothing green
but tended and contained.

I'm sounding so like Virgil. I've collapsed —
no *Amores* for his *Georgics*, *Metamorphoses*
for *Aeneid,* that civilized cross-tiled
courtyard between poets sparking
across answers; brick parody graunches
pink under the elegist's too-smooth alabaster.

Nature should be walled, pastured, left
to the sun or what it breeds up in dragon's teeth —
these blank-eyed Goths, walking statues of themselves
of one basalt shade. They're no natural addition;
should be burnt off like couch-grass.

Here my naming collapsed; my sinewed
rhetoric's been evacuated, trope by trope,
from the squares and villas it played on.
I recite in the caldarium of my dreams;
wake to find it recites back. The old
turn-off walls close in with all their once
white-echoing sunlight snuffed in wattle.

Nothing rings, burns them off, warms or breathes
through their dead-march. My days are smoke.
They sting my throat and vanish. I'd pour an oblation
to some idiot ancestor, some rite to observe
the service-worn leather panels of calm and storm;
boredom and border panic that's the only play.
Now, near sixty, I'm finally the cadet I veto'd young;
hobbling after my strayed equestrian blood,
which never counted me in the pulse of noble
generations. I shall leave it a daughter.

I'll stop a barbaric dart more forcible
than the court barb that shaped me
to it. It's not the Roman nose condemns me,
not even sequent emperors, waiving
my petitions with a morbid fart; but
the dead note back from nature. Nothing
in it echoes but a few caverns, ravines
in my fondly-quitted Sulmo through the Abruzzi.
What I mould bounces words off its
stucco or sounding verdegris.

It's not even you thinning readers, but echoes
preserve words in marble veins, statues,
columns, or shot with dice across a polished floor, inlaid
with all the lustral flights of gods I nod to, dreaming,
and forget. Here there's nothing for me but
one tiled stride of fishes; and to draw
them to shore. I was born at the cusp of
Pisces. They rule the feet.
Let me browse with my webbed toes then,
mesh-net with the scaled mosaic, my last
plummet to artifice to wriggle out a truth.

Let them say I died reading with my feet,
that crude square-inlaid artistry
hunkered back these few words. Picture
me at last a native here; a shore-delving
Neptune with his appetite back.
Someone you could set round its rim,
who generations walk over,
whose hard-wearing onyx
some could just take in.

Notes

Notes on the Poems

No Bees, No Planet [p.2]
Taking the slogan of the time catches an early 2007 response to a now commonplace fear. At the time, all kinds of theories enriched suggestion; years on, the swarming exit remains a constant.

Morlocks [p.4]
Very broadly, the poem adopts some themes from H. G. Wells' *The Time Machine* (1895). It was also made into a film in 1960, some details updated to fit 1895-1966 (the latter itself now a dated projection of imminent nuclear war, allowing a glimpsed 1917 character to return, old and unbelieving, to confront the unchanged Traveller). The Traveller discovers, in the year 802,701, a bifurcated human species after some catastrophe: 'Morlocks' and 'Eloi' . The former live underground, brutish, crudely technophilic cannibals; the latter simply their pretty Edenic cattle frolicking above. I'm not suggesting those of us tubing it will turn into Morlocks, even on the Northern. That's the goverment's prerogative.

24 Hour Dream People [p.10]
Such a title inevitably suggests *24 Hour Party People*, on which the dream is based. Boethius (c.480-525) who wrote *The Consolations of Philosophy* whilst awaiting execution by Theodoric (who repented of it too late) was invoked in this biopic of the Haçienda, by a tramp played by Chris Ecclestone. In Chaucer's *Troilus and Criseyde* Boethius takes Troilus up after death to look laughing down on his tribulations; a striking use of Boethius as embodying his philosophy. Tony Wilson's singular vision informs the film and this version of events, which is thus tainted. In the context of dream-distortions, perhaps it's right it should inform the psychosis of dream. Thus personal memories — my mother really did live in a house in Cyprus, but the shower is certainly refracted — distort with it.

1348, by St George [p.17]
1348 twins the ousting of Edward the Confessor for the Capadocian St George as Patron Saint of England, by Edward III. It curiously coincided with another gift from the east, the Black Death.

Aftertaste [p. 18]
George Bush Sr. shot down in his TBF Grumman Avenger (camouflaged midnight blue, silver grey, and white), was rescued by a passing U. S. submarine. He was lucky to avoid being eaten — by a cannibalistic Japanese lieutenant, who consumed allied airmen and soldiers. He was hanged. Osaka is very fine imitation single malt Scotch, distilled by the Japanese from 1924. Taste striations separate more on the tongue. Germany's version is the next best, for the same reason. Bush Sr. later met the Christian Japanese soldier who'd named his own son after the cannibalised U. S. airman he'd befriended. Bush Sr. hated going to war, and as Timothy Garton Ash said in a *Guardian* strapline of April 3rd, 2008: 'Europe owes a huge thank you to skilful, patient President George Bush' (bar one might add the disastrously unsupported Iraqi Marsh Arab and intellectuals' revolt of April 1991). He then added: 'I refer, of course, to Bush the father... Pity about the son.'

June 24th, 1967 [p.20]
This is the date of the greatest British pot-holing tragedy and many peoples' worst nightmare. Ten cavers entered Yorkshire's Mossdale system on the morning of the disaster. Four returned, found a storm outside, with flooding, and raised the alarm. It took 18 hours and stream-diversions to locate, eventually, all six bodies of the cavers, who were buried in the High Level Cavern.

Homage to Adrian Mitchell [p.26]
It humbly essays an obvious homage. Mitchell wasn't here to write new invectives. Someone had to.

Old Times [p.29]
A touring version of Pinter's 1971 play *Old Times* was staged at Brighton's Theatre Royal in early March 2007.

The Tiers of St Martin's [p.30]
The poet Sophia Wellbeloved told me her experiences in a previous incarnation, as it were, as tutor of painting and sculpture at St Martin's School of Art from the 1970s and '80s.

Patrick Garland's *Brief Lives* [p. 31]
The director Patrick Garland wrote his one-man television piece for Roy Dotrice in 1964, adapting it for the stage in 1967. This Brighton Theatre Royal February 2008 revival (replacing the obviously *Reluctant Debutante*, which finally came out three years later) still starred Dotrice, then 83. It's so enduring that I saw another version (their second) mounted by Lewes Little Theatre, October 2009, starring and directed by Dudley Ward. Garland himself gave an engaging talk in November 2010, to Sussex Playwrights.

Decline and Fall [p.33]
This piece is based on a part of the career of Will Mason (b.1960), who with his partner Gillian paints everything from murals of the Royal Botanical Gardens at Kew and the set of *The Duchess*, for which they received an Oscar, to Will's work on easels. This is best apostrophised as a kind of stripy figurative mannerism, quite unique; think Wyndham Lewis portraits, Dali, and the striped proto-Fauvist palette of Roderic O'Connor. When the oil runs dry, Will suggests that in oil states at least, the princes will revert to ancient wandering without glancing back. This seems extraordinary, but other witnesses agree.

For the Autochrome Archives of Albert Kahn, 1908 [p. 35]
In 2007 BBC4 mounted a series of programmes on this remarkable banker philanthropist's attempts to document the world in colour photography from 1909 to 1931. Cine film lagged in black and white till the 1920s. Kahn commissioned many world-class photography teams. Dying bankrupt in 1940 at 80 (thus escaping Nazi persecution), he saw his legacy preserved, now belatedly celebrated.

Richard Euringer (1891-1953) [p.37]
Euringer was a minor German and major Augsburg poet, somewhat eclipsed by the very different Brecht. Euringer wasn't a Nazi quite, but was complicit. His prim relatives keep an ultra-conservative café that my translator Gerald Fiebig brought me to as a typical act of cultural provocation.

On the Morning of Milton's Nativity [p.39]
This records the same period as 'Sussex Eye', when I spent an appropriate time nearly blind, trying to see Fiennes' *Oedipus*, over Milton's 400th.

The Distinguished Thing [p.43]
Henry James never dined in at his own house for 30 years. So my own family being on his dining circuit was hardly that distinguished. The title is taken from his famous last words, when he keeled over with a stroke in March 1916. 'Ah, death, the distinguished thing.' Possibly the best exit line since Goethe, but equally possibly he'd rehearsed it.

Clowns [p.44]
My family had brewing connections with Bremen through Amsterdam and, with a family of acting friends connected, like them, with brewing and acting. They owned a tiny horse that somersaulted upstairs. Jewish, they had little chance to emigrate either.

Saving My Skin [p. 54]
Harold Jenner my grandfather undertook a trip of homage to where two relatives survived Gallipoli, in 1925. The bare facts are as reported. The surmise made in this poem of April 2007 has since been confirmed by my cousin Miles. Harold perfected bumbling innocence to lie abroad for his country.

The Man who Mistook his Life for a Hat [p. 56]
Title naturally adapted from Oliver Sachs. Harold Jenner again. Alan Cobham's Circus offered flights for five shillings, loops for ten. Beerbohm's masterpiece *Enoch Soames*, recounts Beerbohm's encounters with the eponymous anti-hero, the one fictional element in an 1890s memoir first published in 1916. Soames — drooping in a wide-awake hat — sells his soul to the Devil on June 3rd, 1897, the Diamond Jubilee, to be projected into the British Museum that day hence in 1997. He'd then look for the tomes on his three slim volumes. The Devil knew of course that all he'd find bar three catalogue labels was Beerbohm's tale of him, suggesting he never existed. 1997 is projected as a comic

Wellsian dystopia. Beerbohm ingeniously prophesied Soames would come again from Hell that day, so exhorted preparations. The BM obligingly mounted a Soames Day to persuade Soames' anguished soul that he was remembered. He was caught on monitors and discreetly applauded.

Venus Flaring [p.76]
A poem populated with two famous translators who might just be happier remaining (at least partially) anonymous. The 'you', a third person altogether, now living in Italy, might prefer to as well. But the author of the title shouldn't be: I stole this from Suzannah Dunn, whose fifth novel's title this is, and who doesn't mind.

O Julia, Assiduae multis odium peperere querelae [p.78]
This is from Propertius 2:18a, the opening line, translated as: 'constant quarrels have led to hatred for many' (tr. Vincent Katz, Princeton University Press, 2004). I've added the Propertian invocation and changed the name from his Cynthia to Julia, equally a Roman one.

Satyre VI: Suffer the Street Children [p.84]
Donne at least accepted the St Paul's Parish Commission for the deportation of street boys to the Americas. In 1621 this was tantamount to sending them to almost certain death, and indeed all died. Donne wrote five Satyres early in his career, and this impertinent imagined Sixth addresses self-accusation.

Asymmetry [p. 86]
A 12h century Islamic scholar learned in mathematics, astronomy and poetry was common. Omar Khayyam (1048-1131) was a better mathematician than poet. Al-Haytham or Alhazen (965-c.1040) was the greatest physicist of his age, a supreme pioneer of optics (the passage of light, point of a convex mirror, camera obscura) and scientific method.

We now recall Crusader politics as infinitely more complex than simple outrageous invasion. Some Crusaders formed alliances with the Turco-Persian Sunni Seljuk states of the 11th-14th centuries. Others factioned with other Sunnis or Shias. This set Crusaders against each other. Outremer (the French outre-mer;

'overseas') was the generic for the Crusader states established after the First Crusade of 1095: the County of Edessa (1098-1149), the Principality of Antioch (1098-1268), the County of Tripoli (1104-1289) and especially the Kingdom of Jerusalem (1099-1291).

Licence and prohibitions on women inevitably differed not only in religion but state. Broadly, Islamic women could own property outright from the 8th century, if sometimes only a third of an estate. In Britain the Married Woman's Property Act came in only in 1882. European women could engage in trade and live uncloistered — think Wife of Bath — but were deemed vessels of lust. Female sexuality, if strictly cloistered and owned, was though celebrated in much of the Muslim world. Eleanor of Aquitaine partly imported it back around 1154 from returning knights as *fin'amor* to liberate the wholly misogynistic West. Though ducal courts seem to have bubbled in a version of it from around 1099 with the First Crusade. One synchronicity: Urban II who ordered the First Crusade in 1095, in the same year ordained married priests sell their wives into slavery, use his Vatican brothels to slake lusts and fill coffers. A Crusade against women and sexuality it took Eleanor to strike the first blow against, armed with a most unexpected Islamic revenge.

Baghdad, the greatest, most cultured city of the world after its founding in 732, was sacked several times in the 11th century. Nevertheless it wasn't the Christians just yet, who sacked it with full massacres: the Mongols in 1258 destroyed it, setting back Islamic civilisation terribly; and Tamurlane trashed it in 1401. The 2003 invasion occasioned huge cultural loss, only partly self-inflicted.

Black Sea Letter Book V [p.88]
Another effrontery. I'd not read Pushkin's imaginary monologue in the guise of someone who'd known Ovid, though not really who he was, until after I'd written this in 2007.